MW01231599

French Home Cooking

80 Easy Recipes Cookbook for Preparing At Home Traditional and Modern French Dishes, Bread and Desserts

By

Adele Tyler

© **Copyright 2021 by (Adele Tyler) - All rights reserved.**

This document is geared towards providing exact and reliable information in regards to the topic and issue covered. The publication is sold with the idea that the publisher is not required to render accounting, officially permitted, or otherwise, qualified services. If advice is necessary, legal or professional, a practiced individual in the profession should be ordered.

- From a Declaration of Principles which was accepted and approved equally by a Committee of the American Bar Association and a Committee of Publishers and Associations.

It is not legal in any way to reproduce, duplicate, or transmit any part of this document in either electronic means or in printed format. Recording of this publication is strictly prohibited and any storage of this document is not allowed unless with written permission from the publisher. All rights reserved.

The information provided herein is stated to be truthful and consistent, in that any liability, in terms of inattention or otherwise, by any usage or abuse of any policies, processes, or directions contained within is the solitary and utter responsibility of the recipient reader. Under no circumstances will any legal responsibility or blame be held against the publisher for any reparation, damages, or monetary loss due to the information herein, either directly or indirectly.

Respective authors own all copyrights not held by the publisher.

The information herein is offered for informational purposes solely, and is universal as so. The presentation of the information is without contract or any type of guarantee assurance.

The trademarks that are used are without any consent, and the publication of the trademark is without permission or backing by the trademark owner. All trademarks and brands within this book are for clarifying purposes only and are the owned by the owners themselves, not affiliated with this document.

Table of contents

INTRODUCTION 5

CHAPTER 1: FRENCH FOOD AT A GLANCE 7

1.1 The Fascinating History of French Food................................. 8

1.2 Historical Facts and Traditional French Cuisine 9

1.3 French Food Specialties by Region 11

CHAPTER 2: FRENCH BREAKFAST AND SNACKS
RECIPES 12

2.1 French Breakfast Recipes.. 12

2.2 French Snacks and Sides Recipes....................................... 24

CHAPTER 3: MAIN COURSES: LUNCH AND DINNER .. 38

3.1 French Lunch Main Courses 38

3.2 French Dinner Main Courses.. 51

CHAPTER 4: FRENCH DESSERTS AND BREAD RECIPES
.... 72

4.1 Desserts Recipes 72

4.2 French Traditional Bread Recipes 85

CONCLUSION... 93

Introduction

French cuisine is known as the base and the core of several delicacies in the World today. In reality, the past of cuisine cannot be put without a large portion of our current history becoming impacted by French cooks. French cooking's power and popularity are iconic and have earned the status of possessing elegance and sophistication. In modern culinary classes and cooking training, the techniques used in French food are commonly taught. In reality, Le Cordon Bleu in Paris, France, is among the globe's most popular and highly respected cooking school.

French cuisine varies from rural, woodsy dishes to intricate, fine dining and all in among. Northern France lies at one end of the scale: vine crushing, salt processing, and slow-roasted stews. The Paris custom of elevated dining is from the other end of the spectrum: rich candies, gold-brushed croquembouche, pickling cucumbers, and deep roux. Next to visual pleasure, there is a heavy focus on flavor and spice in French food. Flattened red Espelette peppers are produced in the Pyrenees, and fleur de sel flakes cover the Region of Biscay's salt mudflats. Even South vineyards make a few of the finest wine and liquor in the country. Furthermore, much farther down the Mediterranean Sea are the lavender lands and olive trees of Provence.

Although the French is renowned for culinary grandeur, there is no need for French cuisine to be picky. The core of French cuisine, in particular, is to emphasize new, high-quality products so that their basic flavors and formulations stand out.

Of course, butter, milk, cheese, and other culinary landmines are the cornerstones of French food, but the plate does not have to be taken over.

French cuisine can also be relatively nutritious; it turned out. France is one of the world's healthful nations with tiny sizes of portions and healthy lifestyles support. However, France is abundant in healthy meals, besides the rich fine cuisine.

"French Home Cooking" is a French recipe book. It has four chapters that discuss French cuisine in detail with all the recipes. Chapter one is about a brief introduction to French cuisine and history. Historical facts and regional influences are also discussed in the chapter. Chapter two is about breakfast and snack recipes. Chapter 3 is about lunch and dinner main courses. In chapter four, you will learn some delicious desserts and bread recipes. Start reading the book now and get yourself ready to prepare delicious French meals to make your day tasteful.

Chapter 1: French Food at a Glance

The core and underlying of many cuisines around the Western world was commonly called French food and preparation. The impact of French Cuisine cooking methods and their appreciation is iconic. That importance is exactly why it can be overwhelming for a novice to learn French cuisine. French cuisine leaves many cooks believing they have to adhere to a certain beauty and elegance unachievable.

The foundation and many other delicacies are commonly called French food and cuisine since the impact of traditional French cooking is delightful. French cuisine may sound complicated, but basically, it is about making a cohesive meal, like the coq au vin of Burgundy. You can understand how to create vinaigrette in a particular way so that you can seek one of the easiest recipes around you after you have perfected the salad, including a poultry boast that is all soft and tender within.

Different courses can be cooked in French feudal food but consumed all at once. The liquids were deep, sweets were a popular commodity, and the buttercream pie was not produced until the Middle Ages. Northeastern France now offers a surprising variety of flavors, concentrating on apples, bacon, and pork. The inhabitants are multi-cultural in Metro France, but they also cook traditional French food with fresh fruits, gratin verts, mushrooms, or dried fruits. Typically, they would prepare local meals, getting a real sense of territoriality. Chicken and sheep, particularly common from early fall to February, are accessible year-round, but France does have a surplus.

1.1 The Fascinating History of French Food

Historically, French cuisine background began with explaining culinary contracts and brief recipes in the middle Ages. Nevertheless, let us skip the Dark Ages and reflect on some of the sweeping reforms that happened after the Revolution and get a better understanding of how French cuisine began in history. Until sugar-mania struck the nation in the sixteenth century, French recipes were commonly acidic-sugar placed in water, vinegar, fish, and meat! In later life, this practice brought about a profound shift in French food patterns: a strong distinction has been made among sweet and salty foods, and at the end of a meal, desserts were regularly served.

In the seventeenth century, French food became a blueprint for other foods, in large part. So first of all, this century has seen people start feeding with a fork! While in areas like Italy, the forks were a popular sharpener, the French thought for years that this was a dumb way of dining and used their hands. Intellectual discourse and reading within France had become a hot button topic. During Revolution, cuisine: food was presented as an artistic medium and debated in peace, science, and religion.

French food had become more available by the end of the eighteenth century, well into the 19th, "cuisine bourgeoise" recipe books became quite famous. Usually chocolatey, rich in beef, spices and baked for periods in boiling jus (flavors), this food was an evolution of court-served aristocratic cooking. Instances of this food are local dishes such as boeuf bourguignon, bouillabaisse, coq-au-vin, and gratin dauphinoise, as well as mother roux sauce.

In comparison, the French Revolution reached a decisive point in the food industry when it triggered the guild members' collapse.

Any French chef could produce and sell any food commodity they desired, with guilds no more operational. This lead to a form of awakening within the French food sector. More gourmet experts have begun to discover numerous pathways for various types of recipes and meals.

French food has undoubtedly lost some of its global hegemons. There are so many exciting outsiders to the global fine dining scene who have exceeded the existing French chefs. The continued success of today's French food is not insignificant.

1.2 Historical Facts and Traditional French Cuisine

France was not keen on herbs, plantains, and mushrooms. Seasoning blends and designs were used until the fourteenth century. France had so many farm food; without lavish ornamentation, it was plain fare. Italy's Catherine de Medici returned to Florence in the middle of the fourteenth century to meet the Crown Prince Henri II, taking with her Florentine-educated chefs and a love of artistic drama and etiquette. French cuisine has developed into a significant art of stunning appearance and creative flavors in the years to come.

In French food, the nineteenth century has carried about drastic changes. The globe cuisine is made popular by its elaborate preparation, and the detailed display is modern haute cuisine. It was the French food processing model before food reviewers contested it for being too rigid. A 1970s reaction against the classic strong French cuisine was the latest cuisine. It loosened up the cream sauce and used fewer products to concentrate on the true flavors. It is noticeable in today's specific French cooking by versatile preparing procedures and further experimenting with non-traditional varieties.

They have an annual average of 46 pounds of cheese for each person. French food is a rare culinary experience that combines elegance, leisure, and medicinal preparation with spicy, healthy foods. Producing and preserving French food is a craft that takes years and years to learn but also needs time to enjoy its glory. Start exploring and accept French cuisine to be an art, a practice, and a mode of living.

For each day of the year, France has a new cheese. Classic French culture makes the love of food a major priority. The French believe that eating is not only a neutral thing but a tradition. In France, often people drink their hot drinks from cups and drop bread or pastry into them. France becomes the world's first nation to ban retailers from tossing away unsold produce to reduce food wastes. Rather, it is donated to charity and other programs through retailers. Per year, France manufactures 10 billion baguettes. People consume nearly 500,000,000 snails per year in France. By rule, there should be just three ingredients for a typical baguette: wheat, yeast, and spice. It must weigh 260 grams as well.

1.3 French Food Specialties by Region

Typically, the French bake and cook recipes local to their country. This does not suggest that they are parochial; the French have a true sense of elegance, and that is why urban French cuisine in France is alive and active. They are likely to taste a wide range of national and regional recipes in metropolitan France. In certain communities around the world, where people are multi-cultural or have diverse ethnic groups, this is real. Local goods depend heavily on traditional French foods. One of the most widely used items is new grapes, grapes, haricot verts, chives, mushrooms, different squash, and dried fruits. Chicken, lamb, beef, and veal are easily accessible year-round, and during hunting that stretches from early fall to February, animal meat is exceptionally common and plentiful. France has an excess of artisanal wine and cheese, no matter the place.

The rich, elegant tastes of mushrooms and ducks and the dramatic spices, peppers, and olives imported from nearby Mediterranean cuisines are featured in Southern France. A fascinating variety of tastes is also offered in Northern France, concentrating extensively on farmhouse-style professions using grapes, milk, beef, potatoes, bacon, and beer.

In traditional French food, the products used and the cooking methods found throughout France vary greatly. One can find a special and traditional cuisine in each area, based on the different customs and prepared foods that have evolved in France.

Chapter 2: French Breakfast and Snacks Recipes

2.1 French Breakfast Recipes

French Cafe au Lait

Cooking Time: 7 minutes

Serving Size: 1

Ingredients:

- ⅔ cup milk
- 2 tablespoons coffee
- ⅔ cup water

Method:

1. In a coffee maker, process coffee and prepare it.
2. Warm the dairy on the stovetop or in an oven to froth the dairy using a French press, then strain it into a French press.
3. To extract hot milk till it increases in length, use the plunger.
4. Use an electronic dairy frothier that warm and foamed simultaneously is the simplest and easiest method of frothing milk at homes.
5. The drink pours coffee and dairy in equal amounts so that you may tailor it to your preference.

Easy French Pain au Chocolat

Cooking Time: 13 hours and 10 minutes

Serving Size: 16

Ingredients:

- 1 and ½ cups cold whole milk
- One 4-ounce bar semi-sweet
- 2 teaspoons salt
- 1 Tablespoon active dry yeast
- ¼ cup unsalted butter
- ¼ cup granulated sugar
- 4 cups all-purpose flour

Butter Layer

- 1 large egg
- 2 tablespoons whole milk
- 2 tablespoons all-purpose flour
- Egg wash
- 1 and ½ unsalted butter

Method:

1. Split the butter into four 1-Tablespoon pieces and put a food processor with the dough hook attached in the pan.
2. Add the rice, salts, baker's yeast. Switch the machine for two minutes at higher speeds to carefully blend the components.
3. Add the milk gently in with the machine running.
4. Switch the machine on to moderate flame until all of the milk is applied and pound the flour for at least five full minutes.

5. The dough is going to be fluffy. It will pull away from the container walls and bounce right back if you prod it with your hand.

6. Take the bread from the pan, then work it into a sphere with lightly oiled palms.

7. From the oven, cut the dough. Start with your palms to flatten out the dough.

8. Move the combination to a lined baking pans mat or a covered baking sheet of paper towels.

9. In the fridge, put the whole sheet pan and cool the buttered surface for thirty minutes.

10. On the rimmed baking sheet, position the folded dough, covering with bubble wrap or plastic wrap, and cool for 4 minutes to cool.

11. Make the croissants form.

12. Preheat the oven to 204C.

13. Mix all the components for the egg wash.

14. From the oven, cut the croissants. Lightly clean each one with egg wash.

15. Bake for twenty minutes until the croissants are nicely browned.

French Omelette

Cooking Time: 15 minutes

Serving Size: 1

Ingredients:

- Freshly ground black pepper
- 1 tablespoon unsalted butter
- 2 tablespoons milk

- Pinch kosher salt
- 2 large eggs

Method:

1. In a large dish, mix the whites, milk, spice, and seasoning and blend well with a spoon or a fork.
2. Set the sheet next to the burner.
3. Heat a thin, prepared omelet tray or non-stick saucepan over medium heat.
4. Insert the butter whenever the pan is hot.
5. Sprinkle the pot as it heats to spread the oil.
6. Add the eggs as the butter begins piping hot, and the bubble dissipates.
7. With a heat-proof spoon, stop to let the eggs warm moderately and then whisk intensely, ensuring that you periodically use the edges of the beaten egg so that the omelet cooks equally.
8. Bang the pot softly on the burner until the ingredients are just set, and remove the pot's omelet.
9. Hold the skillet at an angle of 45 degrees to the oven and shape the omelet.
10. To avoid browning, cook only until the crispiness's optimal degree raises the pan or decreases the steam. Move and serve on a warm plate.

French Baguette

Cooking Time: 3 hours 10 minutes

Serving Size: 60

Ingredients:

- 10 ounces cool water

- Additional flour

- 16 ounces bread flour

- 2 teaspoons kosher salt

- 1 ½ teaspoon active dry yeast

- 1.75 ounces warm water

Method:

1. In a small cup, weigh the hot water and scatter the fermentation on top.

2. Put back to allow the fermentation to become liquid and disperse.

3. Quantify into a large mixing bowl the wheat flour and whisk in the salt.

4. In the middle of the butter mixture, create the well and mix in the yeast that has been absorbed.

5. When cooking, insert the cold water, a few at a time until the flour is stiff and hairy.

6. Use cling film to protect the pot and allow the mixture for thirty minutes.

7. Move the bread to a lightly floured worktop and softly press it into a triangle and divide it into thirds. Switch and loop at 90 degrees.

8. In a wide oiled tub, put the dough and coat it with cling film.

9. Enable it to grow will double in volume in a warm position before.

10. Cut the dough into four equal parts and form each into a bread loaf with vertical sides.

11. Put the loaf on a lightly greased towel, cover them with greased cling film and allow them to grow in volume until twice.

12. Heat the oven to 460 degrees F, and put it on the sheet pan with a water bowl.

13. Reveal the baguettes and pass them to lightly oiled cookie sheets

14. Spray with powder and create four elongated slits with a lame, scissors, or razor blade, one each away.

15. Cook the loaf until crispy and moldy. When pressed, the baguettes can give a hollow tone.

Honeyed Fruit Salad

Cooking Time: 15 minutes

Serving Size: 8

Ingredients:

- ¾ cup cherries
- Optional: 1 kiwifruit
- 2 pears (cored)
- 2 peaches (pitted)
- ½ cup white wine (dry)
- 1 tablespoon sugar
- 1-pint strawberries (hulled)
- 2 tablespoons lemon
- ½ teaspoon zest
- Three tablespoons honey

Method:

1. In a mixer, heat the ingredients till the coating is creamy.

2. Before serving, relax for twenty seconds.

3. Reduce or half the strawberries, slice into ¾-inch sections of pears and berries, and halve the fruit.

4. Lengthwise, split the kiwifruit in the quarter and afterward cut every half lengthways into ½-inch pieces.

5. With the required size of seasoning, mix the ready fruit and serve instantly or cool.

Quiche Lorraine

Cooking Time: 55 minutes

Serving Size: 8

Ingredients:

For the Pie Crust

- ½ cup (125g) butter
- 1 large egg
- ½ teaspoon salt
- 1 ½ cups (180g) all-purpose flour

For Filling

- 1 ½ cups (150g) Emmental cheese
- Salt and pepper
- ½ cup (120 ml) milk
- 1 ¼ cups (300 ml) heavy cream
- ½ onion
- 1 cup (200g) bacon
- 4 large eggs

- 1 tablespoon butter

Method:

1. In a wide pan, mix the flour along with a touch of salt. Before you have a smooth cookie crumb consistency, roll in the oil.

2. To allow the materials to stick well, beat the eggs, shape a solid dough, and sit for thirty minutes in the fridge.

3. Roll a wide wheel and row a 27 cm/ 8.6 inches springs formation on a soft baking sheet.

4. Prick the pizza dough at 350F/180C for fifteen minutes with a spoon and pre-bake this.

5. Fry the onions over medium heat with one tablespoon of oil until the onion is cooked, around eight minutes.

6. For around three minutes, fried the sliced bacon in a deep fryer.

7. The whites, milk, and butter are whisked around.

8. Insert the Emmental shredded cheese. With salt and black pepper, spray.

9. Line the pie crust with the fried onions and insert the sliced bacon.

10. Place the filling over it and cook at 350°F (180°C) in the bottom section of the oven for thirty minutes.

11. Once the pie is perfect and the filler has strengthened, the pie is finished.

12. Caramelize with grated parmesan. Serve hot with the dessert.

French Almond Croissants

Cooking Time: 40 minutes

Serving Size: 12

Ingredients:

For the Almond Cream

- ½ cup almond flour
- 1 tablespoon all-purpose flour
- 1 teaspoon vanilla extract
- ¼ teaspoon almond extract
- ¼ cup granulated sugar
- 1 large egg
- 3 tablespoons very soft butter

For Finishing

- Powdered sugar for sprinkling
- ½ cup sliced almonds

For the Croissants

- 17.25- ounce puff pastry

For the Egg Wash

- 1 teaspoon water
- 1 large egg

Method:

1. Heat the oven to 400 degrees F. With baking parchment, cover a 13x18-inch sheet plate.

2. In a moderate dish, mix the sugar and butter. Mix well with each other! Add the ingredients and egg. When soft, sprinkle again.

3. To mix, insert the almond flour and whisk. Insert the all-purpose flour, then mix until smoother again.

4. In a small pan, mix the egg and one teaspoon of liquid. With a spoon, whisk rapidly until well blended. Just put aside.

5. Break the bread into three equal-sized rectangles using a pastry cutter or razor blade.

6. Break each rectangle into two triangles, one long.

7. Position all of the triangle with both the long edge towards you. At the long end of any triangular, cut a short slit.

8. Squeeze into each triangular two tablespoons of frangipane.

9. Place the frangipane across each right triangle ground.

10. To the remaining frangipane, add one teaspoon of dairy and set it aside.

11. Pour the mixture into croissants, beginning at the long end, spacing the dough out a little at the wide end when you start rolling.

12. With other pie crust layers, repeat this step, then put all of the croissants on the ready cookie sheet, spaced 1 ½ inch apart.

13. Rub each croissant gently but coating all of the bare areas with the beaten egg.

14. Place the mixture in the hot oven and cook for fifteen minutes.

15. Take the condensed frangipane from the furnace and scrub with it.

16. Take and switch to a wire rack from the stove.

17. Enable the croissants to settle, then scatter with the icing sugar for ten minutes.

French Radishes with Salt and Butter on Toast

Cooking Time: 5 minutes

Serving Size: 2

Ingredients:

- Fleur de sel
- Toasted baguette
- 1 European stick butter
- 1 bunch French breakfast radishes

Method:

1. Cut the radishes into large, thinly sliced and use a mandolin or a razor blade.

2. Place a sheet of cheese on top of each piece of toast, cover with radish pieces and scatter with Fleur de Del.

French Toast Roll-Up

Cooking Time: 23 minutes

Serving Size: 8

Ingredients:

- 3 tablespoons butter
- Maple syrup
- 2 teaspoons cinnamon
- Eight slices of soft white bread
- ¼ cup milk
- 2 tablespoons sugar
- 3 tablespoons unsalted butter
- 1 tablespoon ground cinnamon
- 2 large eggs
- 2 tablespoons brown sugar

- 3 tablespoons sugar

Method:

1. Melt three tablespoons of oil in a shallow oven cup until it has just warmed.

2. Mix in two tablespoons of icing sugar, two tablespoons of brown sugar, and one tablespoon of spices with a spoon until a creamy, spreadable blend emerges. Just put aside.

3. Mix the milk and eggs in a small dish. Only put aside.

4. Mix two tablespoons of granulated sugar and two tablespoons of seasoning in a small bowl. Just put aside.

5. Stretch one loaf out to around 1/8-inch thick with a spoon after cutting each piece of bread's crusts.

6. Apply a thin layer of the flour mix on each slice and wrap up firmly.

7. Replace with the leftover flour mix and slices of bread.

8. In a big, non-stick sauté pan, put three tablespoons melted butter and let it melt over medium-high heat.

9. Insert one roll in the beaten egg at a time and place in the saucepan.

10. Enable the roll-ups to sauté until lightly browned and moderately crispy from the outside for two minutes per hand.

11. Transfer to a working surface and gently spray each roll with the combination.

12. Offer with condensed milk instantly.

French Scrambled Eggs

Cooking Time: 10 minutes

Serving Size: 1

Ingredients:

- One tablespoon chopped chives
- Two slices of country bread, toasted
- 3 large eggs
- 3 tablespoons whole milk
- 1 tablespoon unsalted butter

Method:

1. First, beat the egg whites gently in a small cup.
2. Heat the oil in a medium bowl until gloopy, over medium-high heat.
3. Beat the eggs, then cook and stir until set; softly stir in the dairy and chives.
4. Take it off the fire and serve this with buttered toast.

2.2 French Snacks and Sides Recipes

Open-Face Sausage Snacks

Cooking Time: 10 minutes

Serving Size: 8

Ingredients:

- 1 garlic clove, minced
- 48 slices cocktail rye bread
- 2 green onions
- 1 tablespoon prepared horseradish
- 1 package pork sausage
- 1 cup cheddar cheese

- 1 cup Parmesan cheese
- 1 cup mayonnaise

Method:

1. Heat the oven to 375 degrees F.
2. In a large cup, mix all the ingredients, excluding the bread.
3. On a cookie sheet, put slices of toast in a thin layer.
4. Cover with roughly one tablespoon of sausage apiece.
5. Bake for ten minutes or until golden brown gently.

Pizza Pinwheel Snacks

Cooking Time: 32 minutes

Serving Size: 8

Ingredients:

- 24 slices pepperoni
- 1 can pizza sauce
- 2 cups mozzarella cheese
- 1 can roll dough

Method:

1. Heat the oven to 375°F.
2. Squeeze the eight triangles of cone roll pastry into four rectangles on a wide baking tray.
3. With six slices of pepperoni or even quantities of fresh mozzarella, cover each rectangular.
4. Pull lengthwise securely and break into four or more bits together.
5. Cook until lightly browned in the oven and bake, around 12 minutes.

6. For frying, prepare with pizza sauce.

Apple Snack

Cooking Time: 1 hour

Serving Size: 2

Ingredients:

- ½ teaspoon ground cinnamon
- ½ teaspoon coconut sugar
- 1 large apple

Method:

1. In a huge Ziploc small bag, insert the apple slices and scatter the spices and cocoa powder on board.

2. Zip the container and turn it well, guaranteeing that all the cuts are well covered.

3. In a container, put it in the refrigerator and let it cool for at least an hour.

4. Keep for two days in a container.

Unicorn Snack

Cooking Time: 25 minutes

Serving Size: 16

Ingredients:

- 1.75 oz. candy pearls
- 1 tablespoon Unicorn Sprinkles
- 26 candy melts, turquoise
- 26 hot pink candy melts
- 26 lavender candy melts
- 3 cups Original Bugles

- 1 cup white candy melts
- 1 cup pretzel sticks
- ¾ cup cashew halves
- 1 ½ cups mini marshmallows
- 1 cup Rice Chex Cereal

Method:

1. In a thin layer, scatter oats, pretzels, and peanuts on the baking pans.
2. Put the candy melts of lavender, bright pink, and turquoise in individual resealable plastic containers but do not shut them down.
3. Put it for 30-seconds in a a microwave at fifty percent power.
4. Defrost softly with fingertips and proceed to heat in 30-second increments, at 50 percent strength, until fully melted.
5. Wrap and snap the tips from the bags.
6. Toss the cereal, bagels, and peanuts onto the baking dish.
7. Put the bugles in a large mixing bowl to blend.
8. Heat to melts white sweets at 50 percent capacity for 60 seconds in a small pan.
9. Mix well enough and proceed to warm at 50 percent power in 20-second intervals until fully melted.
10. Put on the bugles and blend properly to coat uniformly.
11. Place and dust with sprinkles on a casserole tray.
12. Break off the combination of cereal, bagels, and cashew nuts.

13. Place the unicorn heads and the seed solution in.

14. Mix in pancakes and serve in colorful paper cups.

15. Store some leftover food in an airtight jar.

Peanut Butter Power Snack

Cooking Time: 10 minutes

Serving Size: 12 bites

Ingredients:

- ½ cup ground flax seeds
- 2 tablespoons honey
- ½ cup semi-sweet chocolate chips
- 1 cup old fashioned oats
- 2/3 cup creamy peanut butter

Method:

1. In a large dish, mix all five ingredients. Mix to combine.
2. To make them easier to roll, put them in the fridge for thirty minutes.
3. Form into 12 bits and prepare for up to one week in the refrigerator.

Santa's Snack

Cooking Time: 5 minutes

Serving Size: 7 cups

Ingredients:

- ½ cup peanut butter chips
- ½ cup vanilla or white chips
- ½ cup raisins
- ½ cup holiday milk chocolate
- 2 cups chow Mein noodles
- 1 cup honey-roasted peanuts
- 2 cups Honey-Nut Cheerios

Method:

1. Place all of the components in two broad-mouth quart cans.

2. Customize it with string and silk.

3. Measure into a cup to eat and mix to blend.

Banana Cereal Snack

Cooking Time: 10 minutes

Serving Size: 3

Ingredients:

- Peanut butter
- 1 cup Cereal
- 2 Bananas

Method:

1. Slice the bananas first and split them into parts.

2. Then pour the grain on the parchment paper, spread the butter mostly on the banana, and place the grain on the peanut butter fruit.

Apple Sandwich Snack

Cooking Time: 5 minutes

Serving Size: 1

Ingredients:

- 2 slices apple
- 2 tablespoons granola
- 1 ½ tablespoons peanut butter

Method:

1. Cover one-half of one apple slice with whipped cream; cover with granola.

2. To complete the slice, put the remainder of the apple slice over the granola.

Mini Cornucopia Snacks

Cooking Time: 15 minutes

Serving Size: 12

Ingredients:

- Glue gun
- 12 waffle cones
- 1 oz. the container of honey cashews
- 3 yards of ribbon
- 1 package cheddar crackers
- 1 cup yogurt-covered cranberries
- 1 package pretzel crackers

Method:

1. Mix the parmesan potato chips, pretzel bagels, blueberries filled in yogurt, and cashew nuts in a dish. Just put aside.

2. Pin the string into 12 bows and stick the waffle poles with a glue machine to create the cornucopia.

3. Then add in the cracker mixture with each cornucopia.

Pizza Cup Snack

Cooking Time: 40 minutes

Serving Size: 32 appetizers

Ingredients:

- 2 ounces turkey pepperoni
- 1 cup shredded mozzarella cheese
- ¼ cup finely chopped onion
- ¼ cup green pepper
- 1 can (8 ounces) pizza sauce
- 2 tubes crescent rolls

Method:

1. Preheat the oven to 375 degrees.
2. Differentiate the dough pipes into eight rolls each; break the rounds in half.
3. Push dough on the base of small cupcake pans sprayed with oil on the edges and up.
4. Spoon pasta sauce through each cup.
5. Add tomato, bell pepper, pepperoni, and sausage and scatter.
6. Cook until the slices are golden brown and cheese melt.

French Onion Soup

Cooking Time: 80 minutes

Serving Size: 6

Ingredients:

- 8 slices French bread
- 1 ½ cups of Swiss Gruyere
- ½ teaspoon black pepper
- 2 tablespoons brandy
- 2 bay leaves

- One tablespoon of fresh thyme
- 6 large red or yellow onions
- 8 cups of beef stock
- ½ cup of dry vermouth
- 4 tablespoons olive oil
- Salt
- 2 cloves garlic
- 1 teaspoon of sugar
- 2 tablespoons butter

Method:

1. Warm three tablespoons of canola oil in a 5 to a 6-quart dense saucepan over medium heat.
2. Insert the vegetables and mix with the canola oil to coat.
3. Cook the vegetables until tender, continually stirring, for around 20 to 30 minutes.
4. Boost the temperature to a moderate level.
5. Insert the additional tablespoon of olive oil and the cheese and simmer for another fifteen minutes, frequently whisking, before the onions start to tan.
6. Spray with sugars (to assist with caramel flavors) and one teaspoon of salt and cook for another five to ten minutes, until the vegetables are well browned.
7. Insert the chopped garlic and simmer for an additional minute.
8. On the bottom edge of the pan, transfer the vermouth to the pan and scrape up the golden-brown pieces, deglazing the bowl when you go.

9. With more salt, spice to fit, and add fresh black pepper. Dump the leaves of the bay.

10. Cover a sheet baking sheet with parchment paper or wrap while the broth is bubbling and heat the oven with a shelf in the oven's top quarter to 450 °F.

11. Clean gently with olive oil on all sides of the French bread or croissant slices.

12. Put it in the oven and roast for approximately five minutes, until finely golden brown. From the oven, extract and serve hot.

Classic Nicoise Salad

Cooking Time: 55 minutes

Serving Size: 4

Ingredients:

- 2 5 ½-ounce cans Italian tuna
- ½ cup Nicoise olives
- 1 head Boston lettuce
- Six radishes
- ¾ cup = olive oil
- One tablespoon chopped fresh thyme
- Freshly ground pepper
- 8 cherry tomatoes
- ½ shallot, minced
- 2 tablespoons Dijon mustard
- 4 large eggs
- ¼ cup white wine vinegar
- 1 pound red-skinned potatoes

- 2 tablespoons dry white wine
- 10 ounces haricots verts
- Kosher salt

Method:

1. In a small saucepan, add the potatoes, fill with ice water, and sprinkle with salt.

2. Cooked once fork-tender, around five minutes, then bring to a boil over moderate flame.

3. Drain and pass to a small bowl; rain and then let chill with the champagne.

4. In the meantime, put a single marinated water casserole dish to a boil.

5. Cover it with marinated ice water in a pan.

6. Transfer the green beans to the hot water; simmer for two to four minutes before crisp-tender and brightly green.

7. Drain and dive into the ice cubes instantly to chill; rinse and dry thoroughly.

8. Position the eggs in the designated saucepan and cover approximately 1 inch with ice water.

9. Over moderate flame, bring to a boil, then protect, turn off the heat and let sit for ten minutes.

10. Drain, then sprint to relax under the cold spray. Under cool running spray, slice it.

11. In a cup, whisk together the mustard, parsley, vinegar, tarragon, ½ teaspoon salt, and pepper.

12. In a long, steady current, brush in the canola oil until it is caramelized.

13. In a shallow pan, mix the tomato with salt and black pepper to compare.

14. To the potatoes, insert about ¼ cup seasoning and flip. Hard-boiled eggs for a fifth.

15. Organize the top with peas, green beans, radishes, tough eggs, and fish.

16. Load into the seasoning some fluids from the vegetables, then add the tomatoes to the dishes.

French Bistro Salad

Cooking Time: 20 minutes

Serving Size: 6

Ingredients:

- ¾ cup parsley leaves
- ½ cup walnuts
- ½ cup tarragon leaves
- ½ cup chives
- 1 romaine lettuce
- ½ big head green oak

Quick Pickled Eschalots

- 2/3 cup red wine vinegar
- 4 tablespoon white sugar
- 2 eschalots

Dressing

- Five tablespoon olive oil
- ½ teaspoon salt and pepper
- 1.5 tablespoon lemon juice

Method:

1. Stir in the vinegar until the sugar dissolves.

2. Mix in eschalots, then quit before that becomes fluffy or becomes purple for thirty minutes.

3. Shake up a pan of dressing.

4. Put a pile of lettuce on a dish.

5. Sprinkle with about ½ of the coating, and toss them softly.

6. Disperse over fresh spices, hazelnuts, and marinated eschalots.

7. Highly drizzle and more covering. Instantly serve!

Chapter 3: Main Courses: Lunch and Dinner

3.1 French Lunch Main Courses

Chicken Basquaise

Cooking Time: 45 minutes

Serving Size: 4

Ingredients:

- 100g Bayonne ham
- Salt and pepper to taste
- 100ml white wine
- 1kg fresh plum tomatoes
- 1.5 Kg whole corn-fed chicken
- Pinch of caster sugar
- 50ml brandy
- 6 tablespoon of extra virgin olive oil
- 1 bay leaf
- 4 sprigs of thyme
- 3 banana shallots
- 1 large red pepper
- 1 large green pepper
- 2 garlic cloves,

Method:

1. Preheat the oven to 200 degrees C.

2. Begin by slaughtering two arms, two thighs, two breasts, and two chicken legs into eight parts. Get the breasts sliced into two sections.

3. Heat three tablespoons of the oil in a pan, skillet, or casserole dish to cook the mixture.

4. Take from the grill, insert the ham, and fried until crisp and clean on some paper towels.

5. Add the remaining garlic and bay leaf to the pot and stay before it continues to leap before the cut shallots and pepper are added.

6. Cook for thirty minutes on medium heat until the mixture is very smooth and finely caramelized.

7. Insert the flambé and cognac, preceded by red wine.

8. Once you insert the fresh sliced tomatoes, reduce the fluid by half.

9. On medium heat, simmer the sauces for twenty minutes before the tomatoes are molten.

10. With salt and a tablespoon of icing sugar, spice the sauce.

11. Heat and cooking oil in a large skillet pan and cook the poultry on both edges until lightly browned. With salt and black pepper, spray.

12. In the boiling chili sauce, move the chicken pieces, put the frying pan into the pan, and cook for twenty minutes.

13. When prepared, offer a scatter of freshly sliced parsley and fried Bayonne ham with both the Chicken Basquaise.

Coq au vin

Cooking Time: 1 hour 10 minutes

Serving Size: 3

Ingredients:

- ½ pound whole onions
- ½ pound cremini mushrooms
- 2 tablespoons unsalted butter
- 1 ½ tablespoon all-purpose flour
- 1 cup good chicken stock
- 10 fresh thyme sprigs
- 2 tablespoons good olive oil
- ¼ cup Cognac
- ½ bottle good dry red wine
- 4 ounces good bacon or pancetta
- 1 chicken
- 1 yellow onion, sliced
- 1 teaspoon chopped garlic
- ½ pound carrots
- Kosher salt and black pepper

Method:

1. Heat the oven to 250°F.
2. In a big roasting pan, heat the oil. Insert the bacon and bake for 10 to 15 minutes over medium-high heat until golden brown.
3. Transfer the bacon with a rubber spatula onto a pan.

4. In the meantime, on paper towels, spread the poultry flat and pat it dry. Spray the meat with pepper and salt in both directions.

5. Cook the chicken parts in quantities in a thin layer for around five minutes when the bacon is withdrawn, starting to brown uniformly.

6. Add the chicken with the bacon from the plate and begin browning until all the chicken is cooked. Just put aside.

7. Transfer the vegetables, onion, two tablespoons of salt, and one teaspoon of peppers to the skillet and simmer for 10 - 15 minutes over a moderate flame, stirring periodically, until the vegetables are nicely browned.

8. Transfer the garlic, then cook for an additional two minutes.

9. Insert the cognac and place the meat, poultry, and any fluids gathered on the pan in the bowl.

10. Insert the juice, chicken broth, and tarragon and bring to boil.

11. Use a close-fitted lid to protect the bowl and position it in the oven for thirty minutes until the chicken is yellow.

12. Take it out of the oven and put it on top of the grill.

13. Puree around one tablespoon oil and the starch and mix into the sauce.

14. Add the onions that are stored. Transfer the additional one tablespoon of oil to a large marinade pan and fry the mushroom on medium-high heat for ten minutes, till brown and crispy. Add to the broth.

15. Take the stew to a boil, then cook for ten more minutes. To eat, season. Serve it warm.

Barigoule of Spring Vegetables

Cooking Time: 1 hour 10 minutes

Serving Size: 6

Ingredients:

- Cilantro sprigs, for garnish
- Maldon flake sea salt
- Kosher salt
- 1 vanilla bean
- 3 tablespoon sherry vinegar
- Freshly ground black pepper
- 5 whole black peppercorns
- 1 bay leaf
- 4 oz. snow peas
- 1/3 cup fresh peas
- 4 cups vegetable stock
- 10 sprigs thyme
- 4 bulbs baby fennel
- 4 bulbs spring onions
- 6 baby carrots
- ¼ cup olive oil
- 10 cloves garlic
- ½ teaspoon coriander seeds
- 1 bunch pencil asparagus

Method:

1. Get a 6-qt. The steamed water casserole dish to a boiling.

2. Process snow peas, lentils, vegetables, and asparagus until buttery, about two minutes for peas, and three minutes for vegetables and asparagus, operating in batches.

3. Shift the veggies to the ice bath until they are cooled; rinse, discard the asparagus rubber band, and set it aside.

4. Clean over moderate temperature until moist, two minutes, pan dry, and toast coriander powder.

5. Add ¼ cup of oil; roast garlic until crispy, 3-4 minutes, and move to a cup using a rubber spatula.

6. Heat celery and white onions until crispy, ten minutes; combine with cloves in a dish.

7. Insert the cut onions leaves, the reserve, the tarragon, the bay leaves, the black pepper, and the vanilla bean; boil for about thirty minutes until reduced significantly.

8. Strain the product and transfer to the skillet; whisk the vinegar, black pepper in the residual water and continue cooking.

9. Stir all allocated veggies in; cook, wrap, four minutes until veggies are cooked through.

10. Split veggies over the top of bowls and put broth; seasoning with sprigs of coriander and kosher salt.

Chicken Paillard

Cooking Time: 34 minutes

Serving Size: 4

Ingredients:

- 4 (6 ounces) chicken breast

Salad

- 4 cups trimmed arugula
- 8 ounces cherry tomatoes
- 1 lemon, juiced
- ½ tablespoon black pepper
- ½ teaspoon salt
- 1 tablespoon extra-virgin olive oil
- 2 teaspoons lemon zest
- 1 tablespoon red wine vinegar

Marinade

- 2 teaspoons extra-virgin olive oil
- 1 clove garlic, crushed
- 1 lemon, juiced
- 1 small shallot, chopped
- ⅓ cup dry white wine

Method:

1. Press chicken breasts to ¼ thickness on a worktop using a wooden skewer or hard skillet.

2. In a small dish, mix the liquor, one lime juice, shallots, two teaspoons of oil, and garlic. Add the chicken thighs; leave for fifteen minutes to marinate.

3. In a wide cup, mix two lime juice, syrup, two tablespoon olive oil, and lime zest; mix in ¼ teaspoon salts and ¼ teaspoon powder.

4. Add the tomatoes and butternut squash; toss to mix.

5. Heat a high-heat outdoor barbecue and gently oil the fryer, or fire a skillet over medium temperature.

6. Remove the chicken from the marinade; sprinkle with ¼ teaspoon of salt left.

7. On a wire rack grill, cook the chicken once lightly browned and just heated completely, two to three minutes on either side.

8. A center-inserted instant-read temperature gauge can read at least 175 degrees F.

9. Place the chicken on top of the arugula bowl.

Cinnamon Apple Bostock

Cooking Time: 1 hour, 25 minutes

Serving Size: 6

Ingredients:

For the Frangipane

- 1 teaspoon pure vanilla extract
- 1 tablespoon. Calvados
- 1 stick unsalted butter
- ½ teaspoon kosher salt
- 1 cup sliced almonds
- 2 large eggs
- ½ cup sugar

For the Toasts

- 1 1/3 cups sliced almonds
- Powdered sugar
- ¼ cup prepared cinnamon syrup
- ¼ cup apple butter
- 6 slices milk bread white bread
- Nonstick spray

Method:

1. Put 1 cup of almonds and sugars in a bowl and mix until finely chopped. Eggs, sugar, and salt are added and refined into a fine powder.

2. Move the mixture to a container and cool for thirty minutes or until midnight. Drizzle with vanilla and Calvados, crackling to blend.

3. In the middle of the oven, put a shelf and heat it to 375°.

4. With parchment paper, line a broadsheet pan and gently grease the paper with a clean towel.

5. Position the bread on the baking tray and spray the cinnamon sauce freely on both sides.

6. Place one tablespoon of apple sauce on one half of each slice, accompanied by 1/4 cup of almond paste.

7. In a shallow bowl, put the leftover 11/3 cups of sliced almonds.

8. To cover the frangipane layer with nuts, push the ready toast into the nut bowl.

9. Move the bread to the baking tray, almond-side-up.

10. Cook for twenty minutes till the almonds are crispy, and the frangipane is somewhat puffed up and set but still tender.

11. Serve hot or at ambient temperature, scrubbed with icing sugar.

Moules Marinières

Cooking Time: 1 hour

Serving Size: 4

Ingredients:

- Salt
- Pepper
- 4 of mussels
- 1 level teaspoon of flour
- Parsley
- 2 shallots
- 15 tablespoon of dry white wine
- 30 g of butter or margarine

Method:

1. Chop the shallots.
2. Scratch the mussels well enough and clean.
3. Placed them alongside butter, the sliced shallots, and the balsamic vinegar in a casserole bowl.
4. Cover them for several minutes over medium temperature in the sealed casserole bowl. While cooking, blend 2 to 3 times.
5. Pull the mussels from the soup pot as long since they are open, preserving the frying juices. Please put them in one deep dish and keep them hot.

6. Take the juice back to the flame.

7. Combine one teaspoon of starch with one spoon and the same amount of margarine.

8. Mix all from the boiling of the mussels on the flame. For a bit, let it simmer.

9. Place the mussels on. Spray and cover with grated parmesan.

Basque-Style Fish with Green Peppers and Manila Clams

Cooking Time: 25 minutes

Serving Size: 4

Ingredients:

- 12 Manila clams
- 2 teaspoon piment d'Espelette
- 2 tablespoon parsley
- 2 lb. boneless hake
- 1 lb. mild green peppers
- 1 medium Spanish onion
- 1/3 cup extra-virgin olive oil
- 2 cups fish stock
- ¾ teaspoon. kosher salt
- 2 cloves garlic
- ½ cup dry white wine
- 1 tablespoon all-purpose flour

Method:

1. Melt the butter in a 12-inch pan over moderate to low heat.

2. Insert the garlic and cook for 1 minute, stirring regularly, until just browned.

3. To mix, scatter the starch over the cloves and whisk.

4. Apply the wine and simmer for about two minutes, moving quickly, before the slightly thickened and decreases slightly.

5. Transfer the stock of fish and sea salt, then carry the water to a boil again.

6. Insert the tomatoes, onions, and tarragon and scatter on the bottom edge with an even surface.

7. Raise the fire to medium, place the bowl and simmer for about five minutes, till the veggies are tender.

8. Expose the bowl and put the fish parts' skin in a clear layer on top of the veggies.

9. Dip the clams and spice the seafood with salts to fit in between the cutlets.

10. Heat and cook till the middle of the fillets are just translucent, and the clams are free for seven minutes.

11. Spread the veggies on a large baking tray, then put the tuna and clams on board.

12. Put the leftover broth over the salmon and, if using, garnish with grated parmesan and Espelette paprika; instantly eat.

Steak Diane

Cooking Time: 30 minutes

Serving Size: 2

Ingredients:

- 1 teaspoon parsley
- Hot sauce
- 2 teaspoons Worcestershire sauce
- 1 tablespoon scallions
- ¼ cup heavy cream
- ¼ cup veal demi-glace
- ¼ cup Cognac
- 1 garlic clove
- ¼ pound button mushrooms
- Kosher salt and pepper
- 1 small shallot
- ½ tablespoon olive oil
- Four 3-ounce beef tenderloin
- 1 tablespoon unsalted butter
- 2 teaspoons Dijon mustard

Method:

1. Heat the oil in the large pan.
2. Sprinkle the meat with pepper and salt and simmer until finely golden brown on edge, around 1 minute, over medium temperature.
3. Change and bake the medallions for 45 seconds further, then move to a foil sheet and cover.

4. In the pan, add the tarragon and cloves and simmer over medium heat, swirling, once fragrant, for about 20 seconds.

5. Insert the mushroom, sprinkle with salt and simmer for about two minutes, once melted.

6. With a long fuse, extract this from the flame, insert the Cognac and cautiously ignite this.

7. Once the fumes die down, insert the vinegar and yogurt and mix for two minutes over mild heat.

8. Mix the Worcestershire sauce, the green onions, the tarragon in the veal demi-glace, and sprinkle with salt, peppers, and hot sauce.

9. Transfer to the frying pan the beef as well as any leftover juices and transform to cover.

10. Boil until warmed through, around 1 minute. Move the beef to the pans, serve on top of the sauces and eat.

3.2 French Dinner Main Courses

Crepes Suzette

Cooking Time: 45 minutes

Serving Size: 8

Ingredients:

For the Crêpes

- ¼ teaspoon salt
- 1 tablespoon butter
- 2 teaspoons orange juice
- 1 ½ teaspoon orange zest
- 2 eggs

- 2 tablespoons butter
- 1 cup all-purpose flour
- ½ cup less one tablespoon water
- ½ cup milk

For the Orange Syrup

- Four tablespoons granulated sugar
- 4 ounces Grand Marnier
- 16 tablespoons butter
- **Topping**: vanilla ice cream

Method:

1. Collect ingredients.
2. Blend the milk, flour, orange zest, two tablespoons of butter, orange juice, water, eggs, and salts strongly till the mixture is fully smooth; let the mixture sit for twenty minutes in the fridge before creating the crêpes.
3. Stir together the rice, butter, eggs, buttermilk, fruit juice, orange zest, and seasoning for the Crepes Suzette method.
4. Over reduced temperature, melt one teaspoon of butter in a crêpe tray or wide pan.
5. Add three teaspoons of flour to the bowl and mix until it is filled in batter at the container's bottom.
6. Cook the crêpe on tops and crispy under it for ten minutes, or until the crêpe is slightly soft.
7. Flip the spoon under it, remove the sides of the crêpe and afterward softly turn it upside-down into the bowl. Heat for two minutes, then to stay warm, move the fried crêpe to a pan. Repeat the procedure with the mixture that remains. Just put aside.

8. Heat part of the oil in a medium saucepan set over medium-high heat until it fizzes.

9. Spray half the sugar over the melting fat and extract the pan from the flame.

10. Insert half the Grand Marnier, gently treating the pan because of the blaze.

11. To brush all surfaces in the citrus syrup, transfer the crêpes to the tray.

12. Roll or fold the crêpes into quarters into pipes.

13. To produce more citrus syrup, heat the leftover butter throughout the pan, extract this from the fire, and add the sweet syrup and Grand Marnier.

14. Beside each crepe, put a bowl of ice cream and rain the Suzette crepe with both the citrus syrup.

Salmon Rillettes

Cooking Time: 1 hour 45 minutes

Serving Size: 2 cups

Ingredients:

- ¼ teaspoon sweet paprika
- Toasted baguette
- 1 ½ tablespoon lemon juice
- 1 tablespoon extra-virgin olive oil
- ¼ pound hot-smoked salmon
- 1 large shallot
- 4 cups water
- 1 teaspoon black peppercorns
- 1 cup dry white wine

- Five tablespoons unsalted butter
- 1 small onion
- 1 bay leaf
- ½ tablespoon sour cream
- 1 celery rib
- 1 leek, halved lengthwise
- Salt
- Freshly ground white pepper
- 2 tablespoons snipped chives
- 1 tablespoon liqueur
- ½ pound salmon fillet

Method:

1. Spray the anise liqueur with both the fish on a tray and sprinkle with salt and red pepper.

2. Top with cling film and leave to stand for thirty minutes at ambient temperature.

3. In the meantime, put the celery, parsnip, cabbage, bay leaves, coriander seeds, vinegar, and liquid to boiling in a medium skillet. For 25 minutes, simmer.

4. To the pot, insert the fish, cover, remove from heat; leave it for ten minutes.

5. Cover the fish, remove some bay leaves, and chill in the fridge for about 45 minutes until it is cooled. Flake some fish.

6. Crumble one tablespoon of the oil in a pan. Insert red onion and simmer until soft, over medium heat. Let it cool.

7. In the meantime, mix the leftover four tablespoons of melted butter in a small bowl until creamy. Mix the crème Fraiche.

8. Together with the pickled and roast salmon, insert the chilled shallot, dill, lime juice, canola oil, parmesan, and mix until blended.

9. Rillettes can be flavored with seasoning and sea salt. Serve with pieces of toasted baguette.

The Ultimate Pot Roast

Cooking Time: 3 hours 45 minutes

Serving Size: 8

Ingredients:

- 1 French baguette
- 1 cup gruyere cheese
- 2 tablespoons Worcestershire sauce
- 6 sprigs of fresh thyme
- 3-4 pound chuck roast
- 4 yellow onions
- 4 cups beef broth
- 1 teaspoon kosher salt
- ½ teaspoon black pepper
- 2 tablespoons vegetable oil

Method:

1. Heat the oven to 325 degrees.

2. The chuck roast is flavored with sea salt, spice, and tarragon.

3. In a bowl, insert the olive oil and heat it.

4. Add chuck and brown, intensely, for five minutes on either side when it swirls and is heavy.

5. Insert the carrots, Worcestershire sauce, livestock broth, and tarragon and simmer for 3 to 3½ hours, sealed.

6. Cover and extract the leaves from the oven.

7. Power on the hi-broil oven.

8. In very big chunks, cut the meat.

9. Pair it with cut baguettes and dairy from Gruyere.

10. Put the bowl in the oven till the cheese starts to melt and smoke, around 1-2 minutes, exposed, and cook.

11. Instantly serve.

Lentil Salad with Pork

Cooking Time: 40 minutes

Serving Size: 6

Ingredients:

- 1 red onion
- Kosher salt and ground black pepper
- 3 tablespoon white wine vinegar
- 3 tablespoon parsley
- 1 rib celery
- 3 tablespoon Dijon mustard
- 1 small yellow onion
- 1 lb. skinless pork belly
- 2 carrots
- 1 lb. lentils
- 6 whole cloves

Method:

1. Stud the garlic with the onions.

2. Top the onions, veggies, pulled pork, carrot, and fennel with 6 cups of water in a big frying pan. Just get it to a boil.

3. To hold a boil, reduce heat and simmer, covered, for fifteen minutes just until the lentils are soft.

4. Thinly slice the celery and vegetables and slice the meat into large ¼ -inch strips.

5. Mix in the vinegar and mustard in a large dish.

6. Transfer the lentils, parsley, spring onion, sugar, and peppers to the veggies, pull pork, and mix to cover. Swap to a cup to serve.

Honey Glazed Apple Pork Roast

Cooking Time: 2 hours and 30 minutes

Serving Size: 4

Ingredients:

- 2/3 cup dry apple cider
- 5 whole sweet-tart apples
- 6 tablespoon. unsalted butter
- 2 medium yellow onions
- 1-2 pork roast
- 4 thyme sprigs
- 4 rosemary sprigs
- 2 tablespoon honey
- Kosher salt and black pepper

Method:

1. Warm the 350°oven. In a wide casserole dish, put the meat and sprinkle with salt.

2. Rain over the pork with the sugar, then scatters the top with the thyme.

3. Sprinkle the oil over the meat, then place the onion from around pig meat in the bowl.

4. Load the vinegar into the skillet and roast until the temperature gauge placed in the center of the meat reads 120°, around 45 minutes, for instant reading.

5. Disperse the apples from meat and bake until the apples are soft and the meat is nicely browned, and the temperature gauge reads 160°, about forty more minutes.

6. Take the pan from the oven and enable the meat to sit for 20 minutes.

7. Move the meat and cut it into small slices on a large plate.

8. When eating, sprinkle the fried onions and apples from around meat and rain with the cooking liquid.

Provençal Stuffed Squid

Cooking Time: 1 hour

Serving Size: 4

Ingredients:

- Wild arugula leaves, for garnish
- Lemon wedges, for serving
- 1 ½ lb. cleaned medium squid
- 1 cup white wine
- Cheyenne pepper

- 2 teaspoon lemon zest
- 12 oz. chard or spinach
- 4 anchovy fillets in oil
- 4 garlic cloves
- Kosher salt
- 2 teaspoon chopped thyme
- ½ teaspoon chopped rosemary
- Five tablespoon olive oil
- Freshly ground black pepper
- 3 tablespoon parsley
- 1 large onion
- ¼ cup dried bread crumbs

Method:

1. Caramelize the chard in hot boiling water for two minutes, quickly rinse and cool underwater flow.

2. Try squeezing the chard until fully dry and cut it thinly. Just put aside.

3. Add the remaining tablespoon of coconut oil over medium-high heat in a shallow skillet.

4. Insert the toast crumbs and simmer for two or three minutes, regularly flipping, until golden brown and buttered.

5. Take the skillet from the fire and leave to cool the bread crumbs.

6. Put three tablespoons of canola oil over moderately high heat in a pan.

7. Insert the onions, sprinkle with salt, and roast for about ten minutes until finely colored and melted.

8. Add the garlic, tarragon, thyme, smoked paprika, anchovies, and cloves.

9. Cook for about two more minutes, mixing. Move the mixture of onions to a dish.

10. Add the fried chard, scraps of preserved bread, and lime juice. With a rolling pin, blend well. Taste the spice and change.

11. Rinse the squid well and wipe it off with ice water.

12. Fill each squid body with a teaspoon, trying to take care not to overfill it.

13. With a toothpick, fix the lower part. Season the filled squid appropriately with salt and black pepper on both hands.

14. With pepper and salt, prepare the tentacles individually.

15. Heat and cook cast-iron pan for five minutes over moderate flame.

16. Load 1 tablespoon of olive oil into the pan, add the squid, and roast for about 4 minutes, turning once until nicely browned.

17. Insert the tentacles from around limbs, and the wine would be applied.

18. Cover with a lid, and simmer for about two minutes till the squid heads and tentacles are soft yet solid.

19. Reveal and continue cooking till the wine is slightly reduced, about a further two minutes, and add salt and pepper.

20. To a wide baking tray, move the squid bodies and tentacles.

21. Disperse around the squid with both the butternut squash and serve with shredded cheese.

Mussels with Herbed Vinaigrette

Cooking Time: 35 minutes

Serving Size: 6

Ingredients:

- Kosher salt

- Piment d'Espelette

- The rind of ½ preserved lemon

- Juice of 1 lime

- Two sprigs of flat-leaf parsley

- 2 sprigs tarragon

- 2⁄3 cup olive oil

- 4 whole chives

- 6 ½ lb. mussels, cleaned

- 1 ½ cups dry white wine

- 2 tablespoon vegetable oil

- 2 cloves garlic, minced

- 6 whole shallots, minced

Method:

1. Steam the duck fat over moderately high heat in a frying pan.

2. Insert the parsley and cloves, and simmer for about five minutes until melted but not golden brown.

3. Raise the temperature to medium-high, insert the liquor and mussels and shield them.

4. Cook for five minutes, moving the pan slightly before the mussels expand. Dispose of those that do not open.

5. Move the mussels to a work surface utilizing tongs or a spatula.

6. In a shallow saucepan, drain the boiling fluid through a sieve and scrap the parsley and cloves into a large dish.

7. Take the remaining liquid to steam and simmer for about fifteen minutes before decreased to ¾ cup.

8. Remove the plate from the fire and let it cool off entirely.

9. In the spring onions and cloves, add ¼ cup of the reduced liquid, then insert the canola oil, the dill, the tarragon, the estragon, the lime juice, and the lemon zest.

10. Toss once mixed well. Dress with salts and pigment d'Espelette.

11. In each mussel, detach and dispose of the hollow top cones and pass the bottoms to a large plate.

12. Over the mussels, drip the vinaigrette and serve with rice.

Lyon-Style Chicken with Vinegar Sauce

Cooking Time: 1 hour

Serving Size: 4

Ingredients:

- ¼ cup crème fraîche
- Herbed Steamed Rice
- 1 cup Banyuls vinegar

- 2 cups chicken stock
- 12 large garlic cloves
- 1 bay leaf
- 3 tablespoons olive oil
- Salt and pepper
- Three tablespoons unsalted butter
- One 4-pound chicken

Method:

1. Heat the 450° oven. Add the oil to a big, dark pan.

2. Season the poultry with salt and black pepper, transfer to the skillet, and cook over medium-high heat until golden brown.

3. To cover the meat, add three tablespoons of oil to the pan and stir.

4. Change the chicken skin sides back and add the cloves and green leaf.

5. Move the pan to the oven and cook the poultry for ten minutes, until all the chicken bits are just clean. Move the parts of the breast to a tray.

6. Transfer the liquor to the pan, bring it back in the oven and roast the leftover chicken for fifteen minutes more, frying it a few minutes, before cooked through.

7. To the pan, pass the meat and cloves.

8. Put the chicken broth to the pan and simmer until decreased to 1 ¼ cups, about ten minutes, carefully remove the golden-brown pieces.

9. Mix in the crème Fraiche and two teaspoons of oil left.

10. Transfer the meat, including any leftover liquids, to the pan.

11. Simmer over medium-high heat, basting several times, till the sauce is mildly thickened and the chicken is cooked through around three minutes.

12. Mix with salt and pepper and eat with boiled herbed beans.

Veal Roast Blanquette

Cooking Time: 2 hours 30 minutes

Serving Size: 8

Ingredients:

- 1 package green peas
- 2 egg yolks
- ½ pound mushrooms
- Two tablespoons all-purpose flour
- 1 pound potatoes
- ½ pound white onions
- ¼ teaspoon dried thyme
- 4 carrots, halved
- 4 pounds veal shoulder roast

Method:

1. Over moderate flame, dark roasted on all surfaces in an 8-quart Dutch oven.

2. Transform tarragon and two cups of water. Then reduce heat to medium, bring to a simmer for thirty minutes.

3. Transfer the vegetables, onions, and potatoes to the bowl.

4. Cover and cook for thirty minutes. Toss in the spores. Wrap, and boil thirty minutes until its veggies and veal are soft.

5. Remove the veggies and bake, and stay warm.

6. Stir the flour and two tablespoons of water in a bowl until combined without any lumps. Stir the mixture steadily in the Dutch oven.

7. Beat the egg yolks in a tiny cup. Mix in any spicy gravy in limited amounts.

8. Slowly dump the combination of egg yolk away into the gravy and stir until it thickens. Serve the remainder of the gravy.

Beef Bourguignon

Cooking Time: 3 hours 15 minutes

Serving Size: 6

Ingredients:

- 1 pound brown mushrooms
- 2 tablespoons butter
- Two tablespoons fresh parsley
- 2 bay leaves
- One beef bouillon cube, crushed
- 2-3 cups beef stock
- 12 small pearl onions
- 3 cups red wine
- 2 tablespoons tomato paste
- 1 pinch salt and pepper
- 2 tablespoons flour

- 1 teaspoon fresh thyme
- 1 large white onion, diced
- 6 cloves garlic, minced
- 1 tablespoon olive oil
- 3 pounds beef brisket
- 1 large carrot
- 6 ounces bacon

Method:

1. Sauté the meat over medium-high heat in 1 tablespoon of oil in a wide saucepan or pan for around three minutes, before crispy and golden.
2. Move to a stir fry bowl of six quarts (liters).
3. Cover dry meat with a clean cloth; grill in loads until all oil sides are golden brown.
4. Move and transfer the vegetables and tomatoes to the stir fry pan with the pork.
5. To mix, sprinkle with ½ teaspoon fine salt and ¼ teaspoon ground black pepper, mixing well.
6. Load the wine into the pan or skillet and let it boil for five minutes, then stir in the starch before lumps are free.
7. Significantly decrease and sweeten it, then put it together with two cups of stocks, tomato sauce, cloves, bullion, and spices into the crockpot.
8. To blend all of the products, incorporate well.
9. Heat for six hours on high-temperature settings or 8 hours on a medium heat setting, or until the beef is split and soft.

10. Start preparing the mushrooms within the last five minutes of the slow cooker: Warm the butter over medium-high heat in a moderate skillet.

11. Insert the remaining two cloves of garlic and boil until the garlic is aromatic (approximately 30 seconds), then transfer the mushrooms.

12. Heat for about five minutes when periodically rotating the pot to brush with the sugar. If needed, season with salt.

13. Stir in the beef stew and mix it with the liquid before serving.

14. Add fresh parsley to the salad and eat with potato salad, rice, or pasta.

Flamiche Recipe

Cooking Time: 1 hour 50 minutes

Serving Size: 8

Ingredients:

For the Crust

- Ten tablespoons unsalted butter
- 4 tablespoons ice water
- ½ teaspoon salt
- 1 ¼ cups flour

Leek and Bacon Filling

- Two large eggs, lightly beaten
- 1 ½ cups shredded Gruyere cheese
- 1/3 cup whole milk
- A pinch of grated nutmeg
- 2 tablespoons flour

- 1/3 cup white wine
- Salt and pepper, to taste
- ¼ cup crème Fraiche
- 1 large shallot, chopped
- 5 large leeks
- 3 tablespoons butter
- 5 ounces bacon, diced

Method:

1. In a wide pan, mix the flour mixture.
2. Insert the cubed oil and slice the butter into the powder with a pastry knife till the consistency is reached with coarse powder.
3. Add the flour, one tablespoon, and combine till the dough falls along - adding water if required.
4. Move the mixture cautiously to a 10-inch tart sheet and cool for thirty minutes, or until it is solid.
5. Heat the oven to 425° F.
6. Penetrate the edge of the crust with a spoon.
7. Break a parchment paper rectangle about four inches smaller than the pie dish.
8. Cover the bottom with the sheet and fill with ceramic pie pounds.
9. Cook for ten minutes in the oven and bake until it is complete.
10. Remove the paper and scales from the stove and release them.

11. Insert the sliced bacon over moderate heat in a large oven and bake until crispy and lightly browned, around five minutes.

12. Pick the bacon from the plate and use a rubber spatula.

13. Take all but one teaspoon of the bacon fat away.

14. Insert the oil and insert the sliced shallot until melted. Heat for about two minutes, till transparent.

15. To cover them with the oil, insert the cut leeks and mix.

16. Insert the red wine, cover partially, and simmer until the chives are tender, stirring periodically, for around ten minutes. Use pepper, salt, and nutmeg to spice.

17. Insert the bacon back in. Mix in the flour and simmer for a minute or two, stirring continuously.

18. Then add the milk and mix until the mixture thickens. Now add crème fraiche into the mixture.

19. Allow it to cool, and then let it sit overnight from the flame.

20. Then beat the eggs and 1 cup of Gruyere cheese and whisk until mixed.

21. Place the filling solution into the allocated crust to build the pie. Scatter uniformly over the rest of the leftover cheese.

22. Toast for about thirty minutes until baked and well browned.

23. Before serving, let it settle for at least a few minutes.

24. Serve at ambient temperature or hot.

Duck Confit

Cooking Time: 20 minutes

Serving Size: 4 duck legs

Ingredients:

- 2 teaspoons peppercorns
- 2 to 4 cups rendered duck fat
- ½ parsley leaves
- 10 sprigs of fresh thyme
- 1 small onion
- 6 medium cloves garlic
- 4 duck legs
- 6 large shallots
- 1 tablespoon salt

Method:

1. Season the duck legs equally with salts on both sides; put down.

2. Merge parsley, onions, cloves, and tarragon in spice grinder bowl and process until coarsely diced but not puréed, around fifteen pulses.

3. Shift half of the vegetable solution to a non-reactive pan, such as a casserole tray that can match duck limbs snugly and scatter in an even surface.

4. Scatter half of the sage leaves and coriander seeds over the vegetable mix, then place the skin-side duck's legs with an even top layer, pushing them into the vegetable combination.

5. Transfer the residual mint leaves and coriander seeds, accompanied by the veggie combination, spread equally over the duck legs so that the legs are very well covered.

6. Conversely, in a one-gallon zipper-lock bag, combine duck feet, vegetable blend, rosemary, and coriander seeds.

7. Once ready to cook: Change the stove top's middle location and heat the oven to 105°C.

8. Heat the duck fat in either a 3-quart reduced saucer or in a toaster pan.

9. Take the duck feet from the solution and clean out as much of the solution paste as practicable before carefully rinsing the limbs under cold water to remove any ingredients; remove the solution.

10. Tap duck feet clean with towels, then place in a thin layer in a duck fat saucer (if used) to ensure that they are fully immersed in oil.

11. Conversely, place the duck limbs tightly in a shallow baking dish and coat them with molten duck fat to ensure that the legs are fully covered in fat.

12. Cover the tray or serving dish with a cover or sheet of aluminum and move it to the oven.

13. Heat until the duck is fully soft and when stabbed with a serrated knife, meat displays virtually no discomfort, and meat has started to peel away from the lower of the drumstick, 3 ½ to four hours.

14. In its boiling vessel, lift the lid from the oven and cool the duck to ambient temperature, but hold it immersed in fat.

Chapter 4: French Desserts and Bread Recipes

4.1 Desserts Recipes

Crème Brulee

Cooking Time: 4 hours and 50 minutes

Serving Size: 8

Ingredients:

- ¼ teaspoon salt
- 1 ½ teaspoons vanilla extract
- 3 cups heavy cream
- ½ teaspoon espresso powder
- ¾ cup granulated sugar
- 5 large egg yolks

Method:

1. Preheat the oven to 163C.
2. Mix all the yolks and half a cup of sugar syrup. Just put aside.
3. In a small saucepan over moderate pressure, mix the cream cheese, coffee powder, and salts.
4. Take it from the fire as soon as it starts to boil. Incorporate the vanilla powder.
5. Drop about half a cup of warm crème Fraiche and sweep in the egg yolks in a long, steady current.
6. Keep shifting the egg yolks so that they do not scatter.

7. Press and stir the egg yolk solution in a slow but steady stream.

8. In a wide baking tray, put the ramekins.

9. If you are not using one pan big enough, cook them in a few bowls.

10. Split the custard, filled up to the brim, between each ramekin.

11. Cover the pan cautiously with around half an inch of warm water.

12. Choose an oven mitt to move the tray to the oven gently, but the baking tray will be hot.

13. Bake till the sides and cores are fixed and a little spongy.

14. The amount of time depends upon the size of your ramekin.

15. Whenever an immediate read thermometer records 170 °F for a more precise symbol, they are done.

16. Position it on a cutting board for at least 1 hour to settle.

17. Before finishing, put in the fridge, loosely sealed, and cool for at least three hours and up to two days.

18. Spray a thin coating all over the top of the cooled custard with the leftover granulated sugar.

19. Use a cooking torch to crisp up the sugars and eat promptly or lock it in the fridge for up to 2 hours before eating.

Palmier Cookies

Cooking Time: 1 hour

Serving Size: 4

Ingredients:

- 4 tablespoons butter
- 1 cup cane sugar
- 1 sheet frozen puff pastry

Method:

1. Get the puff dough unwrapped.
2. When you have your puff crust then, straighten out the edges with your palms or a wooden spoon, creating an even rectangular.
3. Brush uniformly melted butter and over puff dough.
4. Spray the pastry with a quarter of the sugar, and distribute it uniformly around this one.
5. Roll the dough into a large oval using a spoon, pushing the sugar into the dough.
6. Turn the pastry, then continue the cycle, rubbing with butter and rubbing in the sugar's remainder.
7. Rolling the base of the pastry firmly into the end, beginning in the middle, then move the tops of the sheet to reach in the middle as well.
8. The scale of the rolled will be the same. Cover for about thirty minutes in cling film and relax.
9. Heat the oven to 220 °C. Line the paper towel with a cookie dish.
10. Remove the protective wrap and immediately push one of the wraps on top of another.

11. Shave off the pastry's irregular sides, then cut into ½ - inch (1 cm) pieces. They must look likes hearts that are smashed up.

12. To allow movement, position the strips about 2 inches (5 cm) apart on the baking tray.

13. Bake for fifteen minutes till the sugar is nicely browned, and the sweets are pale yellow, turning them halfway.

Financiers

Cooking Time: 50 minutes

Serving Size: 24

Ingredients:

- ½ teaspoon vanilla extract
- 2 ½ ounces brown butter
- Generous pinch salt
- 4 large egg whites
- ¾ cup and 2 tablespoons sugar
- 5 tablespoons flour
- 1 cup almond or hazelnut flour

Method:

1. Heat the oven to 375F and gently butter the innards of 24 mini puff pastries with warmed, not molten, butter, ensuring that the higher rims of the creases are buttered.

2. Place the almonds or hazelnut mixture, salt, flour mixture in a medium-sized dish.

3. Pour in the whites of the eggs and the extract, then the sugar caramelized.

4. Almost to the tip, complete each incision of the mini puff pastry.

5. To level the tips, tap the tins firmly on the oven, then cook for ten minutes until golden brown.

6. If possible, let the financiers heat them in the cartons, cut them, and use a paring blade to help free them.

Apple Cranberry Galette

Cooking Time: 45 minutes

Serving Size: 12

Ingredients:

For the Pastry

- 6 tablespoon sour cream
- ½ cup ice-cold water
- ¾ teaspoon salt
- 12 tablespoon unsalted butter
- 6 tablespoon white cornmeal
- 2 teaspoon. sugar
- 1 ¾ cups all-purpose flour

For the Filling

- 1 ½ cups fresh cranberries
- 2 tablespoon unsalted butter
- ½ teaspoon ground cinnamon
- 8 large apples
- ½ cup sugar
- 3 tablespoon honey
- 3 tablespoon fresh lemon juice

- ½ cup water

Method:

1. Mix the rice, cornstarch, salt, and sugar in a mixing bowl to produce the pastry.

2. Disperse the cubes of fat over the edge and rotate until the fat bits are the peanut peas' size for few more seconds.

3. Mix the creme fraiche and the crushed ice in such a little pan.

4. Sprinkle and pulsate the paste over the flour until the mixture is soft and adheres together.

5. Press the dough into a ball, roll it in cling film, and chill for twenty minutes.

6. In the meantime, mix the syrup, water, butter, lime juice, and spices in a large skillet over medium heat to make the sauce, and bake, swirling, until the sugar is dissolved.

7. Mix in the sliced apples and cook for approximately five minutes before the apples start to soften.

8. Move the apple slices to a cup that used a rubber spatula.

9. In the frying pan, transfer the walnuts to the fluid and cook until they begin to rise about two minutes.

10. Move the cranberries to the container with the apple and use a rubber spatula.

11. Reduce the heat to moderate and simmer the water, then spoon over the fruits until substantially decreased.

12. In the center of the oven, put two racks and heat them about 400 °F.

13. Split the dough. Pull each quarter out into a circular about 12 inches in length on a thinly floured surface and pass to different baking sheets.

14. Split the fruit's filling evenly between the rounds of pastry and distribute it in an equal layer, keeping a 1 ½ -inch border exposed.

15. Over the berries, cover the border.

16. Over the uncovered fruit lie the fat strips.

17. Dust the cookie rims with sugar.

18. At the halfway point, cook the galettes, turning them 180 degrees, till the pie is lightly browned and the apples are soft, 40 to 45 minutes.

19. Move the pans to the wire rack and allow the galettes on the pan to cool fully. With crème fraîche, eat.

French Fig Tart

Cooking Time: 1 hour 10 minutes

Serving Size: 9

Ingredients:

- 1 teaspoon vanilla extract
- ½ teaspoon lemon juice
- ⅛ teaspoon salt
- 1 egg yolk large
- 1 ½ cup all-purpose flour
- ¼ cup powdered sugar
- 4 oz. butter unsalted

Custard Filling

- 1 teaspoon vanilla extract

- 1 lb. (4509 g) fresh figs
- ½ teaspoon lemon zest optional
- ⅛ teaspoon salt
- 2 eggs large
- ¼ cup whipping cream
- 1 teaspoon lemon juice
- 3 tablespoon all-purpose flour
- ¼ cup sugar
- 4 tablespoon butter

For the Glaze

- 1 tablespoon honey

Method:

1. Just for a moment, cream the sugar and butter just until mixed.
2. Insert the vanilla, egg white, and salts and blend well.
3. Finally, fold the flour together - fold when mixed.
4. In the cling wrap, create a disk and tie.
5. In the fridge, cool the bread for at least 2 hours until it is strong to roll.
6. Now use your hands to push the flour into the bowl to lift it toward the tops.
7. At 190 C, heat the oven.
8. Utilizing parchment paper or plastic, line the cooled dough.
9. Use pie weights to fill the interior of the shell.
10. Cook for 20 minutes, till the edges tend to brown slightly.

11. Add eggs and sugars to a cup. Rigorously whisk until it is light and soft.

12. Next, apply the rice, lime juice, sweetness, vanilla, and softened butter.

13. Place the cream and a sprinkle of salt in it.

14. Pour just about 2⁄3 of the remaining space left for the figs into the partly baked pie.

15. As well as you can, organize the cut fruit into the pie. The figs will fall in even more as the mixture boils.

16. At 180 C, cook in an oven and bake for around 35 to 40 minutes until the surface looks fixed.

17. For a glossy glaze, spray the hot figs with sugar.

Parisian Flan

Cooking Time: 30 minutes

Serving Size: 12

Ingredients:

Flan

- 4 egg yolks
- 1 egg
- 6 tablespoons cornstarch
- 1 cup 35% cream
- 3 cups milk
- 1 vanilla bean
- 1 cup sugar

Crust

- ¼ cup milk
- 1 egg yolk

- ¼ teaspoon salt
- ¾ cup cold unsalted butter
- 1 tablespoon sugar
- 1 ½ cups all-purpose flour

Method:

1. Put the cream, sugar, vanilla beans, and peas to boiling in a frying pan.

2. Remove from the heat and protect and leave for ten minutes to steep.

3. Dissociate the cream cornflour in a pan with a brush.

4. Add the entire egg yolks and shells. Slowly pour in the flavored milk.

5. Cook over medium heat, mixing vigorously with a rolling pin or slotted spoon until the paste thickens and covers the slotted spoon, taking care to scrub the underside of the plate. Remove from intense heat.

6. Straight on the milk, cover with cling film, and let chill in the fridge or over an ice bath. Just put aside.

7. Mix the rice, salt, and sugar in a mixing bowl.

8. Insert butter and pump until it becomes the beans' width, a few moments at a time.

9. Insert egg yolk and dairy and trigger until a ball starts to develop.

10. Roll out the pie and cover a 20 cm (8 inches) in length and 6 cm (2 ½ -inch) wide grease pan on a floured surface.

11. Place it in the fridge for fifteen minutes or thirty minutes in the refrigerator.

12. Heat the oven to 200°C with the racks in the highest spot.

13. Pour the refrigerated custard onto the crust.

14. Cut the extra dough down to ½ cm from the stage of the custard.

15. Put on a baking tray and cook until the custard is just mildly wobbly, or for around 45 to 50 minutes.

16. Preheat the oven to broil and emulsify for roughly five minutes just until the custard layer is partly charred.

French Chocolate Bark

Cooking Time: 1 hour

Serving Size: 4

Ingredients:

- ½ cup apricots, ½-inch diced
- ¼ cup golden raisins
- ¼ cup crystallized ginger
- ½ cup cherries
- 1 cup whole salted cashews
- 7 ounces bittersweet chocolate
- 7 ounces chocolate

Method:

1. To 325°, heat the oven. On a sheet lined with parchment paper board mounted on a baking sheet, create a 9 x 10-inch rectangular that used a pencil, then switch the parchment around.

2. Place the walnuts on some other cookie sheet with one surface and cook for 8 minutes. Set to chill aside.

3. In a glass cup, put the semi-sweet cocoa and half the wistful chocolate in an elevated microwave for thirty seconds.

4. Use a slotted spoon, mix. Heat up and stir in intervals of 30 seconds until the cocoa is simply melted.

5. Add the rest bittersweet chocolate instantly and let it come to room temperature, frequently stirring, until it is smooth.

6. On the baking parchment, pour the molten cocoa and gently scatter it onto the drawn rectangular.

7. The correct sequence, scatter the top equitably: first the ginger, then all the cooled walnuts, the cranberries, the dried fruits, and the raisins.

8. Put aside for two hours until firmly formed.

9. The bark can be sliced into 18 to 20 parts and eaten at ambient temperature.

Pears Belle Helene

Cooking Time: 30 minutes

Serving Size: 4

Ingredients:

- Eight small scoops of vanilla ice cream
- ½ cup chocolate sauce
- 2 ½ cups water
- 4 firm Bosc pears
- ¾ cup granulated sugar
- 2 whole cinnamon sticks

Method:

1. Collect ingredients.

2. In a small saucepan, mix the cinnamon sticks, butter, and half a cup of water.

3. Take the water to a boil, lower the temperature, and steam for five minutes before it becomes nicely browned, and then become a smooth syrup.

4. Shift the temperature to the lowest level and softly sweep until the sugar is thoroughly absorbed into the liquid in the resulting 2 cups of water.

5. Transfer the cooked pears to the solution of sugar syrup and boil for fifteen minutes.

6. By puncturing the fruit's thickest portion, measure the internal temperature with a knife; the parsnips are poached until they are just fried through but not tender.

7. Enable the pears if they are at ambient temperature to settle in the liquid.

8. With a rubber spatula, gently lift the pears from the plate.

9. Represent with a rain of chocolate syrup and two little spoonfuls of vanilla ice cream.

Cherry Clafoutis

Cooking Time: 55 minutes

Serving Size: 8

Ingredients:

- ½ teaspoon. kosher salt

- Powdered sugar

- 1 tablespoon amaretto

- ¾ cup all-purpose flour
- Softened butter
- ½ cup granulated sugar
- 1 cup milk
- 4 large eggs
- 1 ½ cup tart or sweet cherries

Method:

1. Preheat the oven to 350 ° and transfer butter to a 9-inch circular baking dish.
2. Scatter the cherries with an even portion of the plate.
3. Add an egg and sugars in a mixer and process until foamy.
4. Add amaretto, milk, flour mixture and mix until smooth.
5. Spill batter over the fruit.
6. Bake until white, about thirty-five minutes, and a piece of wood inserted in the center comes out dry.
7. Serve hot, or sprinkle with icing sugar at ambient temperature.

4.2 French Traditional Bread Recipes

Crusty French Baguette Recipe

Cooking Time: 3 hours 10 minutes

Bread Loaf Size: 60

Ingredients:

- 10 ounces cool water
- Additional flour

- 16 ounces bread flour

- 2 teaspoons kosher salt

- 1 ½ teaspoon active dry yeast

- 1.75 ounces warm water

Method:

1. In a small cup, weigh the hot water and scatter the yeast on it.

2. Put aside and give the fermentation to be watery and disperse.

3. Quantify into a large mixing bowl the wheat flour and whisk in the salt.

4. In the middle of the dry ingredients, create a well and mix in the dissolved fermentation.

5. Transfer the cold water, slightly at the moment, while mixing, till a stiff, bushy dough has shaped.

6. Use cling film to protect the container and allow the mixture for thirty minutes.

7. Move the flour to a gently floured worktop and softly push it into a shape and divide it into quarters. Switch and loop at a 90-degree angle.

8. In a wide oiled pan, put the dough and coat it with cling film.

9. Enable it to grow to almost double volume in a warm position before.

10. Cut the dough into four equal parts and form it into a long bread with toes pointing.

11. Put the bread on a lightly oiled towel, cover them with greased cling film and allow them to grow in volume until twice.

12. Heat the oven to 470 degrees F, and put it on the sheet pan with a pan of water.

13. Reveal the baguettes and pass them to cookie sheets that are lightly greased.

14. Spray with powder and make four elongated slits with weak scissors or razor blade, one each away.

15. Toast the loaf until crispy and stinky. When pressed, the baguettes can deliver a hollow tone.

Julia Child's French Bread

Cooking Time: 8 hours 25 minutes

Bread Loaf Size: 3 small loaves

Ingredients:

- 2 ¼ teaspoons salt
- 1 ½ cups warm water
- 3 ½ cups all-purpose flour
- Two ¼ teaspoons active dry yeast

Method:

1. Mix the fermentation, 2½ cups of the flour mixture in the bowl, and mix the stick blender using a flat beater.

2. For around thirty seconds, blend on medium.

3. Put in hot water. Till a bushy dough emerges, begin stirring.

4. Clean up the beater and turn to the hooks for the dough.

5. Use a few at a period in the remaining cup of flour mix a pie crust, including more or less powder as required.

6. Knead for five minutes with the dough. It should be flat on the top, and the dough would be fluffy and very sticky.

7. Turn dough on a grinding surface and rest for two or three minutes while the bowl is cleaned and dried, and sprayed with anti-stick spray.

8. Transfer the flour to the bowl and mix and then let it rise, sealed, before 3½ times its original length, at ambient temperature. That is probably going to take about three hours.

9. Flatten the dough softly and add it to the pan.

10. At ambient temperature, let the dough rise once it has not yet tripled in thickness, around 1½ - 2 hours.

11. In the meantime, ready the growing surface: roll the flour on a baking tray onto a canvas or cotton towel.

12. Cut the mixture into three chunks.

13. For five minutes, divide each piece of dough in half, cover loosely, and then let the parts rest.

14. Cut into the loaves.

15. With liquid, mist the loaves. Use the hot oven rock to move the loaves into the cooker and transfer a cup of water to the stove tray.

16. Bake once lightly browned for about twenty-five minutes.

17. Spray the loaf at 3-minute periods three times with distilled water.

18. Before slicing, chill for 2 - 3 hours.

Traditional (Real Deal) French Bread

Cooking Time: 4 hours 30 minutes

Bread Loaf Size: 2 loaves

Ingredients:

- 1– 2 cups lukewarm water
- ½ cup water
- 1 tablespoon yeast
- 1 tablespoon salt
- 4 cups flour

Method:

1. Place one tablespoon of fermentation and ½ cup of lukewarm water to a boil in a dish. Just put aside.
2. Combine 4 cups of flour in a wide dish.
3. Place Yeast mixture into the seasoned flour, and use a spoon, mix, and apply an extra 1½ cup hot water until dough develops and pulls away from the sides of the pan.
4. Flour the worktop gently, and pour it out for kneading.
5. Knead for two minutes or before you have an identifiable ball.
6. Start kneading the dough, but this method will be unique to kneading your usual quarter turn.
7. Pour the mixture out onto the kneading sheet and straighten it out of the dough with your palms to remove all the aerosols.
8. Split into two separate parts. Place each part in a ball and rest for five minutes.
9. Take one part, flatten out all the gases with your fingertips.

10. Pick the top and fold 2/3rds back on the bread, secure the bread on itself, use your palm.

11. Fold and close again. Replicate.

12. Lay flat once again, however this time, drop back to the bottom, locking the top to the lower part.

13. Finally, taper off the edges of the dough by gently rubbing your palms with a touch of pressure at the edges to shape a traditional French bread look.

14. Position the face of the bread seal on your sofa, allowing a bit of room for the loaves to stretch between both two while also helping it.

15. Cut it into 3 slices.

16. Protect it with the remaining towel, and let it grow for an hour.

17. Peel the sofa back gently from the loaf and position them softly on either a baking tray or a paddle to position on the baking block.

18. Use a pastry wipe to brush the tips of the raised dough with cool spray.

19. Throw a half cup of water into the base. Position and cover the loaf in the oven.

Gluten-Free French Bread

Cooking Time: 23 minutes

Bread Loaf Size: 2 medium loaves

Ingredients:

- One tablespoon unsalted butter
- Cooking oil spray
- 1 tablespoon honey

- One teaspoon apple cider vinegar
- ¾ cup warm water
- 1 egg white
- 1 ¾ cups gluten-free flour
- 2 teaspoons instant yeast
- ½ teaspoon kosher salt
- ¼ cup tapioca starch
- ¾ teaspoon xanthan gum

Method:

1. Put the grain, tapioca starch, xanthan gum, and fermentation in the mixing bowl fitted with such a whisk attachment, and toss to combine properly.

2. Insert the salts and, to mix, swirl again.

3. In the middle of the flour mixture, make a well and add more water, white eggs, sugar, syrup, and oil, and blend to combine.

4. Shake the paste with the whisk attachment for around a minute at the moderate flame with the stick blender.

5. The dough's going to bunch up. "Enhance the number to moderate and keep beating until the dough starts to adhere to the mixer bowl's edges and looks textured, "smacked.

6. Move the dough to a firmly sealed jar with a cover, seal, and place in the fridge for thirty minutes.

7. Put the cooled dough out on a level surface, thinly brushed with tapioca, once you are able to shape the flour.

8. Lightly brush the dough's surface with far more tapioca, switch it over a couple of times and softly whisk to clean the dough.

9. Cut the mixture into two equal parts using a big knife or bench sharpener.

10. Work with one slice of dough at the moment, brushing with more powder very gently if required to avoid sticking, turning the loaf into a shape, scratching together to secure any gaps in the bread.

11. Turn the dough outward first and then back into it as you turn your hands away from each other, along the sides of the bread, in a quarter movement.

12. The outline should be broader in the middle, trimmed toward the edges.

13. Position the formed rolls on a parchment rimmed baking sheet a few inches away.

14. Wrap and put in a hot, draft-free atmosphere with lightly oiled cling film and make it grow to around 150% of its current length until it has grown. It may take longer to rise in a dry, cold climate, and less time in a wet, moist climate.

15. Do not put it in a hot oven, lift it to some level, or you possibly kill the yeast.

16. Remove from the oven and serve hot.

Conclusion

French food currently rides a thin line among versions of Haute and nouvelle. The attention being paid to its consistency, taste, and beauty is pure and makes every bit a memorable moment. There is just so much variation with French food, which is the most important quality it does have. French food is now known all over the world because of its elaborate preparation and correct performance. By rendering the regular meal and a result of art, it keeps high in attention and reverence.

French food has undergone many changes in growth, contributing to its prestigious status. They developed their type of cuisine into flavorful, elegant, and stylish dishes. French cooking is a sign of heritage. It is no wonder that the French remain well, lean and slender with all of this strong flavor. Today, the flavor is the biggest coup in French food. With a spoonful of rich gravy, freshly captured fish, vivid vegetables, and fruits flavored with aromatic herbs; nibble portions of delicious desserts, all of which are essential components of French food. French Home Cooking is a complete guide to French cuisine and its famous and easy recipes. Try these recipes now and make delicious French meals.

CPSIA information can be obtained
at www.ICGtesting.com
Printed in the USA
BVHW050002090421
604476BV00004B/825